Everyday Forces

David Byrne

Acknowledgements

Illustrations
All illustrations by Andy Parker.

Heinemann Educational Publishers
Halley Court, Jordan Hill, Oxford OX2 8EJ
a division of Reed Educational & Professional Publishing Ltd

OXFORD MELBOURNE AUCKLAND
JOHANNESBURG BLANTYRE GABORONE
IBADAN PORTSMOUTH (NH) USA CHICAGO

© Reed Educational & Professional Publishing Ltd 1997

First published 1997

02 01 00 99 98

10 9 8 7 6 5 4

British Library Cataloguing in Publication Data
A catalogue record for this book is available from the British Library.

ISBN 0 435 09561 7   *Everyday Forces* individual copy pack:
                                   6 copies of 1 title

ISBN 0 435 09415 7   Stage E pack: 1 each of 7 titles

Colour reproduction by Reacta Graphics.

Printed and bound in Great Britain by Scotprint.

Contents

What is a force?

There are many different types of force.
Forces can make things move.

Forces can make things stop. Forces are all
around us. We can make forces with our bodies.

What is pushing?

The boy pushes the wheelchair with his hands.

 **Pushing** is a force. We push things when we want to move them forwards.

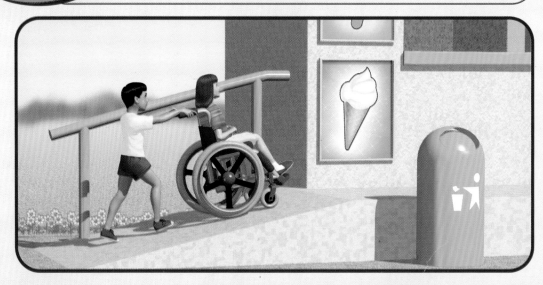

The wheelchair moves forwards.

More force is needed to push something up a slope.

pushing

What is pulling?

The girl pulls the toy caterpillar.

 **Pulling** is a force. We pull things when we want to move them towards us.

The caterpillar moves towards the girl.

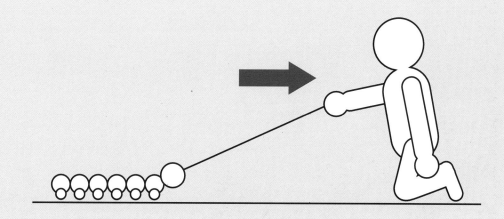

pulling

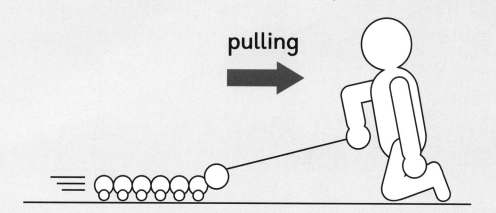

What makes things fall?

The girl lets go of the ball.

 There is a force that cannot be seen. It pulls the ball down. It is called gravity.

The ball falls to the ground.

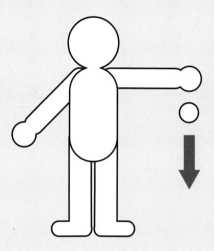

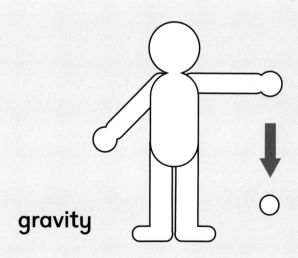

gravity

What makes things stop?

The boy kicks the ball.

Why? The ball rubs against the grass as it rolls. This slows the ball down. The force of one thing rubbing against another thing is called friction.

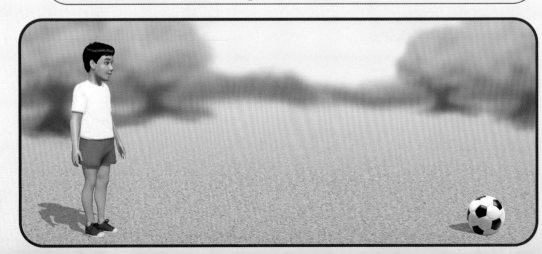

The ball rolls along the ground.
It slows down and stops.

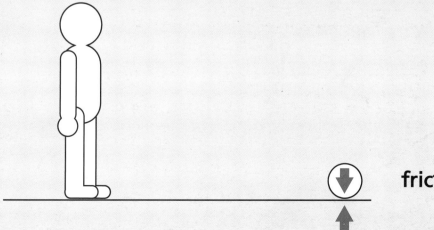

friction

Why do we slide?

1 The girl sits on the slide.

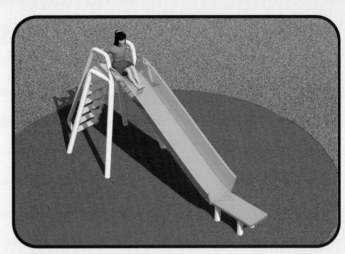

2 She lets go.

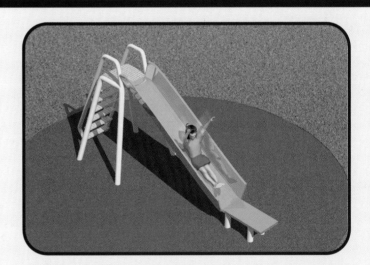

3 The girl slides to the bottom.

She holds on tight.

She goes down the slide.

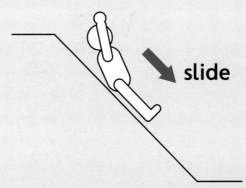

slide

Why? Gravity pulls her to the bottom.

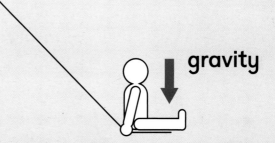

gravity

15

What moves a see-saw?

1 The boy sits on the see-saw.

2 The girl pushes the see-saw down.

3 The girl stops pushing. The boy tips down again.

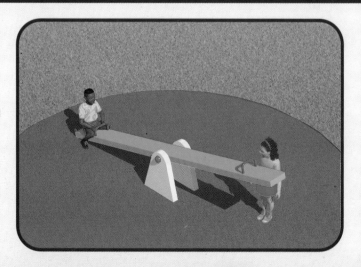

It tips down to the ground.

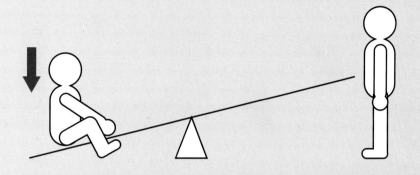

The boy is lifted up.

push

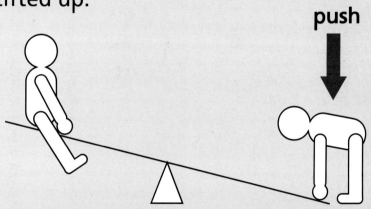

Why? Gravity pulls him down.

gravity

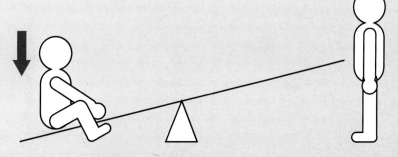

What moves a roundabout?

1 The girl sits on the roundabout.

2 The boy pushes the roundabout.

3 The boy stops pushing. The roundabout slows down and stops.

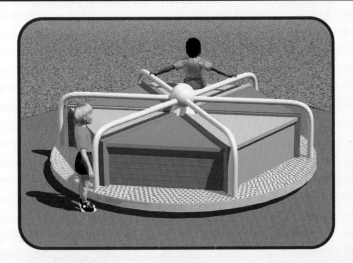

She holds on tight.

It spins very fast.

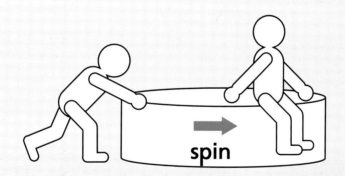

spin

Why? Friction makes the roundabout slow down and stop.

friction

Forces quiz

Can you spot the forces?
Match the words **push**, **pull**, **gravity**, **friction**, to the pictures.

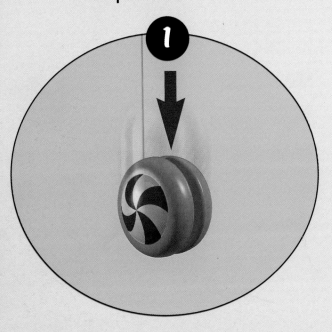

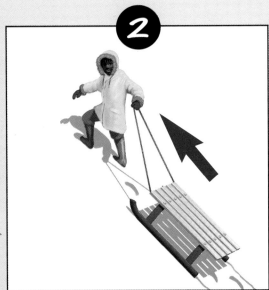

4

5

Glossary

fall

to move towards the ground

force

something which can make things
move, change direction or stop

friction

the force of one thing rubbing
against another thing

gravity

an invisible force which pulls things
towards the ground

move

to make something go from one
place to another

pull

a force which moves something towards you

push

a force which moves something away from you

slide

to move smoothly over the surface of something

spin

to turn around fast

Index